THE HISTORY OF HIP HOP

Volume 1

ERIC REESE

ISBN: 978-1-925988-42-0

For all the real fans of Hip-Hop worldwide!

CONTENTS

INTRODUCTION

What is Hip Hop? The word can mean many things to different people. To some, it is a lifestyle. To others, it is simply a genre of music - revered by some, and dismissed by others. One thing is for sure: Hip Hop has a lengthy history, which audibly and visibly tells the story of thousands of inner-city lives. So, where exactly did it come from?

Hip Hop established its roots in the 1970's in New York City, specifically, largely African-American parts of the Bronx and Brooklyn. DJs were using turntables to create music that was fused from separate records. They would create a rhythm using these "beats" and create lyrical poetry over the spliced sounds to make what is the essential foundation of all hip hop and rap music today.

Since these early days, Hip Hop has expanded quite a bit. While it was originally a form of musical poetry (so to speak), it has developed several subgenres such as "crunk", "gangsta rap", and more. Crunk music, or crunk rap, is a style of Hip-Hop that developed in the southern United States. Its loud anthems and crowd-oriented singalongs are developed specifically to get the dancefloor moving. Gangsta Rap developed in the late eighties in Los Angeles and New York City and was centralized on hard beats which narrated life in the ghetto.

Between the mid-1980s and the early 1990s, hip-hop began to go through a metamorphosis. The art of MCing began to grow as artists started paying more attention to song structure with 4-bar choruses and 16-bar verses, and descriptive narrations in raps.

Early rap pacesetters used wordplay. MCs branched away from end-rhymes rhyming couplets and began different literary approaches such as internal rhyme and chain rhyme. Hip-Hop transitioned from the break beat to characteristics of soul, funk, and jazz.

When major labels began to seek out artists, Hip-Hop drastically grew and entered television media on programs such as MTV and BET. Run from the hip-hop legends known as Run-DMC was once quoted saying, "At a time when hip-hop was becoming really popular in all five boroughs in New York, Bambaataa, Grandmaster Flash, everybody started dressin' up 'cause they had a little bit of money. The Cold Crush Brothers would just come to the parties as is and do their performance."

Since its inception in the seventies, Hip Hop has seen considerable change and evolution. While it comes in many forms, hip hop will always serve as a looking glass to the outside world into African-American culture - for better or for worse. As it continues to change through the 2000's, hip hop will forever stand as both a lifestyle and a style of music which pays homage to its culture throughout over thirty years of history.

1980'S

Rap did not really come in to play until the 1980's because of the dominance of disco. Because of hardships and inequality, young men who had more talent than money put bits and pieces of everybody tracks while putting their poetry on top of their agendas. The B-Boys were from the ghetto, while disco was for the middle class and the rich. But there was hip-hop in both worlds. It was the Hip-Hop tug-o'-war -- disco rappers versus the B-Boys. The '80s marked a new reality: East meets west, with the new, California-based breed seemingly taking their coun-terparts to the cleaners, businesswise and sales wise. The 80's brought a new innovative sound and cultural influence to Hip-Hop community and was known as the "Golden Age" era of Hip Hop. Famous artists from this era include Run D-M-C, Public Enemy, Slick Rick, Salt-N-Peppa, and Big Daddy Kane.

In 1981, Africka Bambaataa revolutionized the sound of Hip-Hop by making an Electro-funk beat to the song "Planet Rock". This fostered similar creativity throughout the Hip Hop world as other artists created their own style of music such as rap group Run DMC, who created "Rap Rock" (A fuse of vocal and instrumental Hip Hop elements combined with forms of Rock-N-Roll). This creative innovation during the 80's is how the name "Golden Age" came about.

In the 1980s, Hip-Hop focused less on the political and marketing aspect on the music industry and more on the lyrical content and overall quality of music. For example, prior to the institution of royalty fees for using snippets of pre-recorded music, rappers were given way more creative freedom because they were able to sample. *"Corporate greed killed the creative music spirit in Hip Hop."*

80'S STYLE

Early female hip-hop artists such as Roxanne Shante, MC Late and Queen Latifah influenced fashion trends for women. Also, the film "Breakin' and Breakin' 2: Electric Boogaloo" showed people what to wear and what slang to say in order to be "hip." Rappers in general during that time wore leather, buttons, bracelets, and chains. Hip Hop artists tended to wear excessive large gold jewelry in the 80's, along with the large outbreak of people wearing basketball sneakers (such as Air Jordans and Adidas shelltops) for recreational and fashionable purposes.

Afro-centrism and the Nation of Islam expanded tremendously in the 1980s, so an increasing amount of African-American males wore Kente cloth. Females in the Hip Hop community wore enormous gold earrings to represent prestige and wealth along with bright neon-colored clothing. Color blocking (design scheme of combining different colors and materials into a single garment) was introduced into the Hip-Hop community in the 80's.

The "Hi-Top" Fade was a very popular haircut in the 80's that was introduced into the urban community.

90'S PURPOSE

"Thematically, hip-hop began pushing beyond the partly rhymes and battle raps that had dominated its early life to include everything from Black Nationalist politics to Five-Percenter ideology to streetwise chronicles of the the criminal underground."

— - YALE (THE ANTHOLOGY OF RAP)

Hip-Hop in the 1990s served as a platform to tell a political and social story or to prove yourself as being an African-American.

90'S INTERPRETATION OF MUSIC

Rakim brought the deeper meanings of rap. The rhythms of Jazz were making their way into music. They used a lot of metaphors. For example, instead of using an deserted image of a drug, Rakim in "Microphone Fiend" creates a song around a metaphor: *"I was a fiend before I became teen, I melted microphones instead instead of cones of ice cream"*. It was one of the best rap songs ever.

THE PLIGHT OF HIP HOP

Hip-hop emerged out of a culture that had an atmosphere of disappointment. After WWII, there were many black refugees that settled in urban centers across America. An urban center in the city of the Bronx, NYC started Hip-hop. Young people also gathered together in parks to rap over sounds and other melodies. Rapping was at the center of this culture, but Hip-Hop was more than just the music.

SOCIAL CONNECTION

Hip-Hop was seen as an outlet for people of color's anger. They were angry because they were poor, black, disenfranchised, abused, ignored, etc. At this point in time, racial tensions were still on the rise. People of color were angry at mainly the middle and upper-class whites because they were mainly denied inclusion in the modern-day's society resulting in unfair wages and good-paying jobs.

POLITICS

Majority of politicians were rich, white males. Issues of segregation were still apparent, though the Civil Rights Era was basically over. Good economic opportunities were very hard to come by in the inner- cities, because all the whites moved out to the suburbs with their big businesses. This caused major issues for the poor who either had to travel long distances to find a good-paying job or resort to working for less wages.

HIP-HOP IS ART

Urban or street art that revolved around Hip-Hop during the 1980s was generally not accepted by the majority. Graffiti is Hip-Hop and police and many community residents saw it as vandalism. What they didn't realize that a new generation of urban folk saw it as art.

MOTIVE

The primary motive behind hip-hop was to express the anger of the people of color with the system and the "man." Artist used their music to draw attention to the plights of social justice and issues that needed to be fixed.

TEXTURE

In the beginning, rap artists generally rapped to artificial beats (beatboxing) and borrowed melodies. It revolved around the production of sounds, not the arrangement of instruments until the late 1970s.

WORLDWIDE

- One of the countries outside the US where hip-hop is most popular is the United Kingdom.

- Hip Hop has globalized into many cultures worldwide, as evident through the emergence of numerous regional graffiti art scenes.

- Hip Hop has emerged globally as a cultural movement based upon the roots of Hip Hop culture; strife and struggle.

- Hip-hop's inspiration differs depending on culture and location.

- All rap artists worldwide have in common is that

they acknowledge African Americans in New York as being the inventors of its art.

- Hip-Hop is sometimes taken for granted by Americans, it is not so elsewhere, especially in the developing world, where it has come to represent the empowerment of the disenfranchised and a slice of getting to the American Dream.

URBAN FASHION

Extra baggy clothes, jerseys, shiny gold jewelry, grills, tank tops, do-rags, tracksuits, bucket hats, basketball caps were the trends in the early days. Nowadays, artists have tattoos, fitted pants, half-shaven heads, track jackets, shirts with sleeves and printed tees, snapbacks, baseball jackets, Jordans, Vans, Nike SB, and hoodies. Artists also have made brands like Gucci, Michael Kors, Fendi, and Louis Vuitton popular amongst the hip hop community.

INNOVATION AND REVITALIZATION

With the use of music distribution through the internet, many alternative rap artists find fans by far-reaching audiences on Soundcloud, Spotify, Amazon and other music distribution channels. Hip Hop artists such as Kid Cudi and Drake have managed to attain chart-topping hit songs, "Day 'n' Night" and "Best I Ever Had" respectively, by releasing their music on free online mixtapes without the help of a major record label.

Wale, J. Cole, Lupe Fiasco, The Cool Kids, Jay Electronica, and B.o.B have been noted by critics as expressing eclectic sounds, life experiences, and emotions rarely seen in mainstream hip hop.

Hip-hop is also used in modern-day rock songs as well.

Kanye West, Jay-Z, OutKast, Tupac, and Eminem are some of the best-selling artists ever. Many of their collaborations involve a combination of hip-hop, pop, soul and R & B artists which has grossed millions.

RISE OF HIP-HOP IN THE 2000'S

- The popularity of hip hop music continues through the 2000s.

- Dr. Dre remained one of the most prominent hip hop figures in producing and beat-making in the beginning of the millennium.

- Dre is the one responsible for the fame of Marshall Mather's (Eminem).

- Hip Hop influences also found their way increasingly into mainstream pop during this period

- Crunk music gained considerable popularity via the likes of Lil Jon and the Ying Yang Twins.

- Jay-Z represented the cultural triumph of hip hop of the 2000s.

- Success of alternative Hip-Hop from groups like the Roots, Dilated Peoples, Gnarls Barkley and Mos Def gained notoriety.

WHAT PURPOSE DOES HIP-HOP SERVE?

Hip Hop gave young black men a voice to be heard especially when media technology started to become more feasible. Rapping also gave some the opportunity to do more than just commit crimes to survive.

Along with focusing on Black Nationalism, hip hop artists often talked about inner-city poverty. This brought a great deal of listeners to the genre who were struggling and coping with the scourge of alcohol, drugs, and gangs in their communities.

Public Enemy's most influential song came out at the time of one of the most plighted times in America called "Fight the Power." The song speaks up to the US government proclaiming that people in the ghetto have the freedom of speech and rights like any other American. One line in the song by Public Enemy, *"We got to pump the stuff to make us tough from the heart,"* grasped the listeners attention and gave them motivation to speak out.

HISTORY: 1925 - 2000

If you start in the past and work all the way to the present, the history of Hip-Hop spreads out in every direction. It dates back to the 1920s when the earliest hip hop dance movements were introduced in the nightclubs and on TV shows. Then it hit the Jamaican dancehall toasting era of the 1950s and 60s. Thus, spreading to the era of the Last Poets and Muhammad Ali and Gil Scott-Heron, who recited poems over beats. Then you had the golden ages of Rakim, Kool G Rap, LL Cool J of the 80s until Nas, Prodigy from Mob-Deep, Jay-Z of the 1990s and currently Jadakiss and Dave East.

1925:
Earl Tucker (aka Snake Hips), a performer at the

Cotton Club, invents a dance style similar to today's hip-hop moves. He incorporates floats and slides into his dance. Similar moves would later inspire an element of hip-hop culture known as breakdancing.

1940:

Tom the Great (a.k.a. Thomas Wong) uses a booming sound system to delight his audience. Wong also utilizes hip American records to steal music-lovers from competitors and local bands.

1950:

The Soundclash contest between Coxsone Dodd's "Downbeat" and Duke Reid's "Trojan" gives birth to the concept of DJ battling.

1956:

Clive Campbell is born in Kingston, Jamaica. (Campbell would later become the father of what we now know as hip-hop.)

1959:

Parks Commissioner Robert Moses starts building an expressway in the Bronx. Consequently, middle-class Germans, Irish, Italians, and Jewish, neighborhoods gradually disappear. Businesses relocate away from the borough only to be replaced by impoverished African-American and Hispanic families. Along with the poor came addiction, crime, and unemployment.

1962:

James Brown records Live At The Apollo. Brown's drummer Clayton Fillyau introduces a sound that is now known as the break beat. The break beat would later inspire the b-boy movement, as breakers danced to these beats at block parties.

1967:

Clive Campbell migrates to the United States at the age of 11. Because of his imposing size, kids at Alfred E. Smith High School nickname him Hercules. He would later become a graf writer and change his name to Kool Herc.

1968:

A gang named Savage Seven would hit the streets of the East Bronx. Savage Seven later changes its name to Black Spades, before eventually becoming an organization known as the Zulu Nation.

1969:

James Brown records two songs that would further influence the drum programming in today's rap music – "Sex Machines" with John Starks playing drums and "Funky Drummer" with Clyde Stubblefield on the drums.

1970:
DJ U-Roy invades Jamaican pop charts with three top ten songs using a style known as toasting. The Last Poets release their self-titled debut album on Douglas Records combining jazz instrumentations with heartfelt spoken word. (The Last Poets would later appear on Common's 2005 rap anthem, "The Corner.")

1971:
Aretha Franklin records a well-known b-boy song "Rock Steady." The Rock Steady crew would go on to rule in the world of break-dancing, with members all across the globe.

1972:
The Black Messengers (a group that staged performances for The Black Panthers and rallies relating to black power movement) feature on The Gong Show.

However, they are only allowed to perform under the alias "Mechanical Devices," because of their controversial name.

1973:

DJ Kool Herc deejays his first block party (his sister's birthday) at 1520 Sedgwick Avenue, Bronx, NY. Herc would often buy two copies of a record and stretch the break parts by using two turntables and mixing in both records before the break ends. The Zulu Nation is officially formed by a student of Stevenson High school named Kevin Donovan. Donovan later changed his name to Afrika Bambaataa Aasim in honor of an ancient Zulu chief.

1974:

After seeing DJ Kool Herc perform at block parties, Grandmaster Caz, Grandmaster Flash, and Afrika Bambaataa start playing at parties all over the Bronx neighborhoods. Around this time, DJ/MC/Crowd Pleaser Lovebug Starski starts referring to this culture as"Hip-Hop."

1975:

Herc is hired as a DJ at the Hevalo Club.
He later gets Coke La Rock to utter crowd-pleasing

rhymes at parties (e.g."DJ Riz is in the house and
he'll turn it out without a doubt"). Coke La Rock and
Clark Kent form the first emcee team known as Kool
Herc & The Herculoids. DJ Grand Wizard Theodore
accidentally invents 'the scratch.' While trying to
hold a spinning record in place in order to listen to
his mom, who was yelling at him, Grand Wizard
accidentally caused the record to produce the "shigi-
shigi" sound that is now known as the scratch.
Scratch is the crux of modern deejaying.

1976:
DJ Afrika Bambaataa performs at the Bronx River
Center. Bambaataa's first battle against Disco King
Mario sparks off the DJ battling that is now
embedded in the culture.

1977:
The Rock Steady Crew (the most respected b-boy
crew in history) is formed by the original four
members: JoJo, Jimmy Dee, Easy Mike, and P-Body.
DJ Kool Herc is nearly stabbed to death at one of his
parties. Although the assault placed a permanent
dent on Herc's career, Grandmaster Flash, Afrika
Bambaataa, Disco Wiz (the first Latino DJ), and
Disco King Mario kept performing around town.

1978:

Kurtis Blow, who was being managed by Russell Simmons, decides to hire Simmons' brother Run, as his DJ. Run was so-called because he could cut so fast between two turntables.

Kurtis would later become the first rapper to be signed to a major record deal.

Music industry coins the term "rap music" and shifts its focus toward emcees. Grandmaster Caz (aka Cassanova Fly) and Bambaataa engage in a battle at the Police Athletic League.

1979:

Grandmaster Flash forms one of the most influential rap groups ever, The Furious 5: Grandmaster Flash (Joseph Saddler), Melle Mel (Melvin Glover), Kidd Creole (Nathaniel Glover), Cowboy (Keith Wiggins), Raheim (Guy Williams), and Mr. Ness (Eddie Morris). Around the same time, another great rap crew – The Cold Crush Four – was formed, comprising of Charlie Chase, Tony Tone, Grand Master Caz, Easy Ad, JDL, and Almighty KG. The first rap record by a non-rap group "King Tim III" is recorded by the Fatback Band. Sugarhill Gang's "Rapper's Delight" would go on to become the first known rap hit, reaching #36 on Billboard. Various obscure rap singles were also released: Grandmaster Flash & The Furious 5's "Super-rappin" and Spoonie Gee's "Spoonin' Rap" both on Enjoy Records, Kurtis Blow's "Christmas Rappin" on Mercury Records, and Jimmy Spicer's 13-minute long storytelling track "Adventures of Super Rhymes" on Dazz Records. Mr. Magic's 'Rap Attack' becomes the first hip-hop radio show on WHBI.

1980:

Afrika Bambaata and the Zulu Nation release their first 12" called Zulu Nation Throwdown Pt. 1 on Paul Winley Records. Kurtis Blow, the first rapper to appear on national television (Soul Train), releases "The Breaks" on Mercury Records. The record goes on to sell more than a million copies. Hip-hop gradually evolves into big business. After meeting Fab 5 Freddy and others, Blonde releases "Rapture" featuring rap vocals by lead singer Debbie Harry.

1981:

Grandmaster Flash releases "The Adventures of Grand Master Flash on the Wheels of Steel," the first record to ultimately capture the sounds of live DJ scratching on wax. On February 14th, The Funky 4 plus One More perform their classic hit, "That's The

Joint" on NBC's Saturday Night Live becoming the first hip hop group to appear on national television. The Beastie Boys are formed. The group consists of Adam Horovitz (King Ad-Rock), Adam Yauch (MCA), Michael Diamon (Mike D).

1982:

Afrika Bambaataa and the Soul Sonic Force release the techno-heavy "Planet Rock" on Tommy Boy Records. The record samples portions of Kraftwerk's "Trans-Europe Express." Grandmaster Flash & the Furious 5 release "The Message" on Sugarhill Records. Kool Moe Dee humiliates Busy Bee in a spontaneous rap battle. Since then, emcee battling has become an inseparable part of Hip-Hop. Fab 5 Freddy and Charlie Ahearn co-produce Wild Style, a hip-hop film featuring Cold Crush Brothers, Grandmaster Flash, Grandwizard Theodore, DJ AJ, Grandmixer D.S.T, graf writers Lee, Zephyr, Fab 5 Freddy, Lady Pink, Crash, Daze, Dondi, and members of the Rock Steady Crew. Wild Style has since inspired several other hip-hop-themed movies.

1983:

Ice T helps pioneer gangsta rap in the west coast with his rapcore singles "Body Rock" and "Killers."

Grand Master Flash and Melle Mel (Furious 5) record the anti-cocaine single "White Lines (Don't Do It)," which becomes a rap hit. Grandmaster Flash later sues Sugarhill Records for $5 million in royalties. The dispute causes the group to break up, signaling the looming danger of corporate control in hip-hop. Run DMC releases "It's Like That" b/w "Sucker MC's."

1984:

Russell Simmons and Rick Rubin team up to launch one of the most important record labels ever, Def Jam Records. Def Jam releases its first record, "It's Yours" by T La Rock, followed by LL Cool J's "I Need A Beat." Hip-Hop discovers that touring is a great way to generate income, as the Fresh Fest concert featuring Whodini, Kurtis Blow, Fat Boys, and Run DMC, reels in $3.5 million for 27 dates. Battle rap assumes the spotlight in hip-hop, as UTFO's "Roxanne Roxanne" diss song attracts over 100 responses. The most popular response came from a 14-year old female named Roxanne Shante. Shante's "Roxanne's Revenge" allegedly recorded in Marley Marl's living room sold more than 250,000 copies. Dougie Fresh (aka The Entertainer) releases The Original Human Beat Box(Vindertainment

Records). Michael Jackson does 'the moonwalk' at the Grammys, borrowing b-boy dance elements from LA breakers.

1985:

Sugarhill Records goes into bankruptcy and is forced out of business. Salt 'n' Pepa make their first appearance on Super Nature's "The Show Stopper."

1986:

The Beastie Boys release Licensed To Ill on Def Jam (executive-produced by Rick Rubin).

James Smith, a native of Houston, Texas, assembles The Geto Boys. The original lineup consisted of MCs Raheim, Jukebox, DJ Ready Red, and Sir Rap-A-Lot.

The group also featured Little Billy, a dancing dwarf who later picked up the microphone as Bushwick Bill. Following a short break-up in 1988, Smith invited local emcee Willie D and multi-instrumentalist Akshun (later known as Scarface) to complete the lineup. The Geto Boys (now made up of Scarface, Willie D, and Bushwick Bill) was a driving force in the evolution of southern rap.

1987:

Following the release of Boogie Down Productions'
Criminal Minded LP, Scott LaRock is shot and killed
in the South Bronx while attempting to settle a
dispute. Public Enemy stuns the world with their
introductory album, Yo! Bum Rush The Show,
signaling the genesis of politically-charged Hip-Hop.
The original members of the group include Chuck D
(Carlton Ridenhour), Flavor Flav (William Drayton),
Professor Griff (Richard Griffin), and DJ Terminator
X (Norman Rogers).

1988:

After years of being neglected by the mainstream
media, hip-hop gets its own show on MTV, "Yo!
MTV Raps." N.W.A pioneers the gangsta rap
movement with their gold album, Straight Outta
Compton. Def Jam founders Russell Simmons and
Rick Rubin part ways; Simmons opts for distribution
through CBS/Columbia Records, while Rubin goes
on to found Def American.
Landmark album releases: Ultramagnetic MC's –
Critical Breakdown, and Big Daddy Kane – Long
Live The Kane.

1989:

After a life-long battle with crack addiction, Cowboy,

a member of Grandmaster Flash's Furious 5 dies at the age of 28. A group of high school friends join the Native Tongues as promoters of the Afrocentricity Movement to make African-Americans aware of their heritage.

These Manhattan-based friends would later form A Tribe Called Quest (Q-Tip, Ali Shaheed Muhammad, Phife Dawg, and Jarobi). A Dallas-based protégé of Dr. Dre known as D.O.C releases No One Can Do It Better. While the album was making rounds on the charts, D.O.C. found himself in a severe car crash. While D.O.C. survived the accident, his vocal career didn't and started songwriting.

1990:

2 Pac joins Digital Underground as a dancer and a roadie.

The "Stretch & Bobbito Show" is launched. Both a Florida record store owner and Luther Campbell are arrested over 2 Live Crew's controversial album, As Nasty as They Wanna Be.

MC Hammer hit mainstream success with the multi platinum album Please Hammer, Don't Hurt 'Em. The record reached and the first single, "Can't Touch This" charted on the top ten of the billboard hot 100. MC Hammer became one of the most successful rappers of the early nineties and one of the first household names in the genre. The album raised rap music to a new level of popularity. It was the first Hip-Hop album certified diamond by the RIAA for sales of over ten million. It remains one of the genre's all-time best-selling albums. To date, the album has sold as many as 18 million units.

1991:
N.W.A's sophomore album N****z For Life sells over 954,000 copies in its first week of release, reaching #1 on the pop charts. The album paves way for many more hardcore rap albums that would follow. Busta Rhymes appears on A Tribe Called Quest's "Scenario." Cypress Hill (B-Real, DJ Muggs, and Sen Dog) release their self-titled debut, and initiate a campaign to legalize hemp. The Notorious B.I.G. is featured in the "Unsigned Hype" column of The Source magazine.

1992:
The police beating of Rodney King. Dr. Dre released The Chronic. As well as helping to establish West Coast gangsta rap as more commercially viable than East Coast hip hop, this album founded a style called G Funk, which soon came to dominate West

Coast hip Hop. The style was further developed and popularized by Snoop Dogg's 1993's album "Doggystyle". The Wu-Tang Clan shot to fame around the same time. Being from New York City's Staten Island, the Wu-Tang Clan brought the East Coast back into the mainstream at a time when the West Coast mainly dominated rap. Other major artists in the so-called East Coast hip hop renaissance included The Notorious B.I.G., Jay-Z, and Nas. The Beastie Boys continued their success throughout the decade crossing color lines and gaining respect from many different artists.

Record labels based out of Atlanta, St. Louis, and New Orleans gained fame for their local scenes. The midwest rap scene was also notable, with the fast vocal styles from artists such as Bone Thugs-n-Harmony, and Twista. By the end of the decade, hip hop was an integral part of popular music, and many American pop songs had hip Hop components.

1993:

A Tribe Called Quest release their third album, Midnight Marauders, featuring a who-is-who-in-Hip-Hop album cover. Dr. Dre's The Chronic attains multi-platinum status. Wu-Tang Clan release 36

Chambers. The line-up consists of Prince Rakeem
(The RZA), Raekwon, Ol' Dirty Bastard, Method
Man, Ghostface Killah, Genius (GZA), U-God,
Master Killa and Inspectah Deck.
Mobb Deep (Prodigy and Havoc) release their debut
LP, Juvenile Hell.

1994:

Nas' first entry, Illmatic goes gold and is widely
received as one of the greatest hip-hop albums ever.
Common releases Resurrection and is lauded as an
intelligent lyricist. Warren G's Regulate: The G-
Funk Era is certified 4x platinum. 2 Pac is robbed
and shot 5 times in a New York recording studio. He
recovers from the shooting. Pac is later sentenced to
8 months in prison.

1995:

Queen Latifah wins a Grammy award in the "Best
Rap Solo Performance" category for her hit "Unity."
2 Pac signs a deal with Death Row Records after
Suge Knight posts a $1.4 million bail.
Eric Wright (Eazy-E of N.W.A) dies of AIDS on
March 20th at the age of 31.

1996:

The Score, a fusion of conscious lyrics with reggae-
tinged soulsonics, becomes The Fugees' biggest
album. The album debuts at No.1 and grabs two
Grammys, thus, breathing a new life into socially
aware Hip-Hop. The Music of Black Origin (MOBO)
Awards are launched in the U.K. The Fugees walk
away with two trophies. Jay-Z drops his highly-
lauded debut, Reasonable Doubt. His "charismatic
rapper" approach would later spawn throngs of
emulators.

24-year old Snoop Dogg and his bodyguard
McKinley Lee are acquitted of the murder of Philip
Woldemariam, a 20-year-old Ethiopian immigrant
gunned down in August 1993. On September 7th,
Tupac Shakur is fatally wounded after sustaining
multiple gunshots as he rode in a car driven by
Death Row Records CEO Marion "Suge" Knight near
the Las Vegas strip. Tupac died 5 days later. His
death rekindled the debate on whether rap
promotes violence or just reflects the ugly side of the
streets.

1997:
The Notorious B.I.G. (born Christopher Wallace), is
shot and killed March 9, after a party at the Petersen
Automotive Museum in Los Angeles. Like Pac's

murder, Biggie's death is still an unsolved mystery. Missy Misdemeanor Elliott redefines hip-hop and R & B with her first album, Supa Dupa Fly. Having broken barriers as a successful female producer, Missy would go on to become the highest selling female rapper of all time. Parent company Interscope Records sells its interest in Death Row Records and severs ties with the label. Chicago MC Juice defeats Eminem on his way to winning the year's Scribble Jam competition. (Scribble Jam is the largest showcase of underground hip-hop in the United States.) Roc-A-Fella sells a 50 percent stake to Island Def Jam for $1.5 million.

1998:

Dr. Dre inks Eminem to his Aftermath imprint. Lauryn Hill's solo debut, The Miseducation of Lauryn Hill, scores her 11 Grammy nominations and 5 wins, including Album of the Year and Best New Artist. "Hard Knock Life (Ghetto Anthem)" marks the beginning of Jay-Z's mainstream breakthrough and helps move 5 million units of Vol 2: Hardknock Life. The chorus is sampled from the Broadway play "Annie." Shyne (born Jamal Barrow) signs a lucrative record deal with Diddy's Bad Boy Entertainment.

1999:

Backed by producer Dr. Dre, Eminem zooms past
racial hurdles and sells 4 million copies of his debut,
The Slim Shady LP. Production duo The Neptunes
(Chad Hugo & Pharrell Williams) dominate the
airwave with a string of radio hits, including Kelis'
"Caught Out There," ODB's "Got Your Money,"
Noreaga's "Oh No," and Mase's "One Big Fiesta."
Their infectious, bling-tinged sound would later
become an unofficial requisite on hip-hop albums.
Dr. Dre puts the west coast back on the spotlight
with his comeback LP 2001.

2000:

Dr. Dre files a lawsuit against MP3-swapping firm
Napster. Congresswoman Cynthia McKinney holds
the first Hip-Hop Powershop summit to address the
various political, economic, and social issues
affecting the youth. DJ Craze wins the Technics
DMC World DJ Championship 3 consecutive times.
Eminem, through the release of his well received
second album Marshall Mathers LP, solidifies his
place as rap's future great. The title sells 1.76-million
copies in its first week and later scores two
Grammys for the rapper.

MOMENTS IN POP CULTURE HISTORY

In the entire brief history of rap music, a few moments have gone—as the saying goes—deeper than rap.

These are not the scenes and headlines that made hip-hop "relevant" as much as the moments where Hip-Hop characters, ideals, and narratives ended up on the front pages of national papers, shifting the American news cycle and making the sounds, lyrics, and faces of the genre as much a story as any great world leader or event. Sometimes, like Bill Clinton calling out Sister Soulja, the moments were gasoline on fire. Other times, they were just a spark on a fuse waiting to be lit, like Dr. Dre making headphones everybody's most essential personal style accessory.

These are moments of protest, of struggle, and of shame. These are moments of pride and of power. These are moments that define the music we so often take for granted, whether it's Kanye saying some shit about an American President, or an American President saying some shit about Kanye—and then campaigning with Jay-Z not long after. From the subliminal moments to the most pronounced, from the film and TV show moments to the moments when the corridors of political power were forced to confront rappers—yes, rappers—these are those times when Hip-Hop splashed into the mainstream, by all means necessary.

Hip-Hop's taken everything from figurative bows thrown to literal shots fired. Yet, they weren't game changers for rap so much as for pop culture, moments of pure, uncut recognition that this isn't just a subculture, or a trend, but pieces of the greater American mosaic. From Kanye to Clinton, from Style Wars to who Wu-Tang's for, these are the 40 Biggest Hip-Hop Moments in Pop Culture History.

The Moment: What happens when a punk band trying to spice up its repertoire attempts to do so by adopting what New York City punk bands—let alone pop culture—rarely ventured to for its hits? You get the first rap video on MTV, in MTV's first month on the air, in their first 90-video rotation, which arrived in the form of Blondie's "Rapture," the entire coda of which is rapped by Debbie Harry. To hammer the point home, Blondie also recruited hip-hop luminaries to appear in the video with them, like Fab Five Freddy (who's name-checked in the song), Lee Quinones, and Jean-Michel Basquiat.

The Impact: "Rapture" came at a weirdly perfect time as it wasn't just the first video featuring rap on MTV but was a video in MTV's first real "rotation," where it stayed for a few months. In other words, eyes from all over the country saw this young white woman doing the "hip-hop" thing.

The Upshot: At the time, it was neither an abomination nor a momentous occasion, but just a weird rock thing that was, if not amusing, then actually fairly cool. The video helped cement Blondie's place as one of the more progressive bands in contemporary rock, and set the precedent for rock embracing hip-hop (and vice-versa).

The Moment: At the beginning of the new decade, Newsweek—then one of two magazines in every

other suburban, middle-class household, along with
Time—released a cover about the anger of rap
music. The editors wanted to choose between two
rap acts: LL Cool J, and Tone Loc. They went
with Loc.

The Impact: Tone Loc didn't become much
"harder" of a rapper than he already "was." The
impact on Loc's career was minimal at best. The
cover's effect on perceptions of rap, however,
wasn't insignificant. To one segment of America, it
was a sign of things to come: Rap and these
rappers are scary, it screamed, so you better lock
away your children. To another segment of
America, it screamed: People who write
newsweeklies know nothing about rap, as
evidenced by their selection of Tone Loc to repre-
sent anger in rap.

The Upshot: To another, much smaller segment of
America, it screamed: Wow, scaring people with rap
is pretty compelling. Let's replicate it! And thus,
thousands of fear-based pieces about the dangers of
angry rappers were born, in a tradition that
continues to this day. Meanwhile, Loc went on to
have one of the most family-friendly careers in
acting as a rapper has ever had, including famously

being talked to by the ass of Jim Carrey in Ace Ventura: Pet Detective.

The Moment: Other stations had played rap before KDAY, but it wasn't until the hiring of Greg "Mack" Macmillan as their program director and afternoon host that everything changed. Mack turned the station into a Hip-Hop powerhouse, recruiting young talent to not only to DJ, but to have their ears to the streets. One such talent pool? The World Class Wreckin' Cru, whose Dr. Dre had started to mix tracks together on a mixer in real time, splicing old tracks into contemporary rap records.

The Impact: The station became one of the most influential outlets for rap nearly overnight, and broke some of the most important records in the history of rap. Moreover, it created the market for rap radio formats, and if hot rap singles begin anywhere, it's on rap format radio.

The Upshot: KDAY would eventually turn over from a rap format station in 1991, and would relaunch as a less-influential version of the original in 2004 as a middle-ground urban contemporary station. More importantly, however, KDAY lead terrestrial radio executives to realize that the rap format would be a crucial one in years to come, spawning the creation of rap radio all over America.

The Moment: Stand-up comedy—great, edgy, stand-up comedy—was still too hot for most televised broadcasts, let alone stand-up by black comedians, who had to overcome major networks' worries about audience pull and standards and practices troubles. Enter Def Jam founder and label head Russell Simmons, who found himself with a production deal at HBO, that cable channel you had to pay extra for, with all the movies, and a few of its own TV shows that you couldn't find anywhere else. Slapping his record label's name on a late-night stand-up hour on pay cable, Simmons found a place to infuse comedians' personas and performances with a hip-hop aesthetic, and create a home for unabated humor that was topical for a segment of the population that had long gone without one. In doing so, Def Comedy Jam was born.

The Impact: While protested by some for what was perceived as offensive content that reinforced negative black stereotypes, the show would go on to receive relatively high marks from TV critics.

The Upshot: Def Comedy Jam not only paved the

way for edgy stand-up comedy on television, but cemented HBO's place in the media world as an outlet for edgier entertainment, period. It also furthered Russell Simmons' status as an entrepreneur of hip-hop outside of the realm of music and gave rise to a host (Martin Lawrence) who went on to a wildly successful career of his own.

The Moment: Academy Award-nominee and Hollywood royalty actor Warren Beatty writes, produces, consults with Suge Knight on, and directs a movie about a California Senator who goes off the rails, beginning to speak his mind and truth to his own power, in the form of cringe-inducing raps, with an all-star rap soundtrack released by Interscope.

The Impact: Like the titular character, the movie was initially seen as a curious and naive attempt by old white Hollywood to reach out to young urban America, both by Beatty's Hollywood peers and casual viewers alike. As it turned out, both parties ended up loving it: Critics gave it generally positive reviews, the soundtrack produced one of the bigger hits of that summer (in the form of Pras, ODB, and Mya's "Ghetto Supastar"), and the unlikely cultural crossover actually, oddly, managed to work out.

The Upshot: While it hasn't aged so well and still can lay claim to one of the most universally reviled endings in '90s movie history, the film grossed $29 million worldwide, and picked up a handful of nominations for Beatty and Jeremy Pikser's screenplay (which only won a minor L.A. critics award, losing out almost universally to Shakespeare in Love or The Truman Show). The soundtrack was certified platinum by the RIAA. The movie was one of Warren Beatty's last great works, as he continues to ease off major projects.

The Moment: MTV rolled out one of the most unlikely pairings in the network's history to present the 1997 VMA for Best Dance Video: Martha Stewart and Busta Rhymes, introduced by Chris Rock as "one [who] knows how to make a really mean pot roast, and the other one is always roasted on pot." Martha showed up in muted browns, looking demure. Busta showed up in a red and gold kimono. "What the dilly, yo?" Busta grinned, as Martha Stewart looked both completely uncomfortable and also massively charmed. Martha talked about dropping some beats—or beets—and Busta shouted out Wu-Tang Clan and the Flipmode Squad. The entire thing was, in a word, surreal.

The Impact: It contributed to part a great year for both music videos and the Chris Rock-hosted MTV VMAs, which got high marks from TV and music critics as a high point in the brief history of the network and its awards ceremonies, and more crucially, MTV found itself encouraged to take bigger risks with pairings like Busta and Martha, especially after 1998's Ben Stiller-hosted VMAs failed to thrill in quite the same way. Enter the '99 VMAs, which were hosted again by Chris Rock, but this time, at the Met Opera, and had more than a few watercooler moments, like pairing the mothers of the Notorious B.I.G. and Tupac, or Lil' Kim and Diana Ross, who would jiggle Kim's pasty-covered breast on the VMA stage.

The Upshot: If, in 1997, you were asked who would spend more time in jail over the next fifteen years, you'd probably get this answer wrong. Busta Rhymes remained one of rap's most popular and eccentric acts, and then got very, very in shape, and stopped wearing kimonos, and ceased being weird (and wonderful, to an extent). He never did hard time. Martha Stewart continued to grow her media and kitchenware empire but did end up going to jail for insider trading. The VMAs fell into decline after the early Aughts, and have yet to reach quite the peak levels of excitement they generated in the late '90s.

The Moment: In 1985, as the holiday shopping season kicked into full gear, commercials for Swatch started appearing in New York City, featuring an unlikely celebrity endorsement: the Fat Boys, performing the song they'd recorded for the occasion, "Swatch Watch Presents A Merry Christmas."

The Impact: After a Swatch-sponsored tour with Run-DMC, Kurtis Blow, and Whodini, the endorsement of the watch-slingers—made possible by the Fat Boys' manager Charlie Stettler, a Swiss national—became one of the most successful cool-kid ad campaigns of all time, and shot the Fat Boys into the forefront of Hip-Hop as one of its most charismatic, charming, and irresistible acts.

The Upshot: The Fat Boys continued to appear in movies and TV shows (Disorderlies, an episode of "Miami Vice") and made some classic records along the way. More importantly, they proved that rappers were as capable of being a celebrity spokesperson as any other stripe, and thus, paved the way for so many of the multi-million dollar deals we know all too well to come.

The Moment: In the Spring of '97, a commercial starts to air for the Gap, featuring a new kind of spokesperson for the mall-sHopping standard of America: LL Cool J. In the spot, LL sports the Gap neck-to-toe. On his head, however, was a hat by a then little-known streetwear brand called FUBU, which stood for "For Us, By Us," given a shout by LL in the lyrics of his rap during the commercial, with those exact words.

The Impact: Executives for The Gap were supposedly furious, once they actually realized what had happened. And here's what happened: FUBU's founder, Daymond John—an old friend of LL's from Hollis, Queens—kept pestering LL Cool J to wear his new clothing line, until LL actually did...to a shoot for his big Gap commerical. Orders for the clothing line exploded, and FUBU became the original monolithic rapper-endorsed streetwear brand, with revenues totaling somewhere around the $300 million mark in 1998.

TERMINOLOGY

Hip Hop music is a musical genre that developed as part of hip hop culture, and is defined by four key stylistic elements - Rapping, DJing/scratching, sampling (or synthesis), and beatboxing. Hip-hop began in the South Bronx of New York City in the 1970s. The term rap is often used synonymously with hip hop, but hip hop also denotes the practices of an entire subculture.

Rapping, also referred to as MCing or emceeing, is a vocal style in which the artist speaks lyrically, in rhyme and verse, generally to an instrumental or synthesized beat. Beats, almost always in 4/4 time signature, can be created by sampling and/or sequencing portions of other songs by a producer. They also incorporate synthesizers, drum machines, and live bands. Rappers may write, memorize, or improvise their lyrics and perform their works a cappella or to a beat.

THE TERM: HIP-HOP

Creation of the term hip hop is often credited to Keith Cowboy, rapper with Grandmaster Flash and the Furious Five. However, Lovebug Starski, Keith Cowboy, and DJ Hollywood used the term when the music was still known as disco rap. It is believed that Cowboy created the term while teasing a friend who had just joined the U.S. Army, by scat-singing the words "hip/Hop/hip/Hop" in a way that mimicked the rhythmic cadence of marching soldiers. Cowboy later worked the "Hip Hop" cadence into a part of his stage performance, which was quickly used by other artists such as The Sugarhill Gang in "Rapper's Delight".

Universal Zulu Nation founder, Afrika Bambaataa is

credited first with using the term to describe the subculture in which the music belonged; although it is also suggested that it was a derogatory term to describe the type of music.

The first use of the term in print was in The Village Voice, by Steven Hager, later author of "A 1984 history of Hip Hop."

SEVENTIES' ROOTS OF HIP-HOP

The roots of hip hop are found in earlier African-American genres of music and traces as far back as pre-colonial Africa. The griots of West Africa are a group of traveling singers and poets who are part of an oral tradition dating back hundreds of years. Their vocal style is similar to that of rappers. The African-American traditions of signifyin', the dozens, and jazz poetry are all descended from the griots. In addition, musical 'comedy' acts such as Rudy Ray Moore and Blowfly are considered by some to be the forefathers of rap.

Within New York City, griot-like performances of spoken-word poetry and music by artists such as The Last Poets, Gil Scott-Heron and Jalal Mansur

Nuriddin had a significant impact on the post-civil rights era culture of the 1960s and 1970s.

Hip Hop arose during the 1970s when block parties became increasingly popular in New York City, particularly in the Bronx, where African American and Puerto Rican influences combined. Block parties incorporated DJs who played popular genres of music, especially funk and soul music. Due to the positive reception, DJs began isolating the percussion breaks of popular songs. This technique was then common in Jamaican dub music and had spread to New York City via the substantial Jamaican immigrant community. One of the first DJs in New York to use dub style mixing was the Jamaican-born DJ Kool Herc, who emigrated to the United States in 1967. Dub music had become popular in Jamaica due to the influence of American sailors and rhythm & blues. Large sound systems were set up to accommodate poor Jamaicans who couldn't afford to buy records and dub developed at the sound systems. Because the New York audience did not particularly like dub or reggae, Herc switched to using funk, soul and disco records. As the percussive breaks were generally short, Herc and other DJs began extending them using an audio mixer and two records.

Turntablist techniques, such as scratching (seemingly invented by Grand Wizzard Theodore, beat mixing/matching, and beat juggling eventually developed along with the breaks, creating a base that could be rapped over. These same techniques contributed to the popularization of remixes as the looping, sampling and remixing of another's music, often without the original artist's knowledge or consent, can be seen as an evolution of Jamaican dub music, and would become a hallmark of the hip hop style. Jamaican immigrants also provided an influence on the vocal style of rapping by delivering simple raps at their parties, inspired by the Jamaican tradition of toasting. DJs and MCs would often add call and response chants, often consisting of a basic chorus, to allow the performer to gather his thoughts (e.g. "one, two, three, y'all, to the beat").

Later, the MCs grew more varied in their vocal and rhythmic delivery, incorporating brief rhymes, often with a sexual or scatological theme, in an effort to differentiate themselves and to entertain the audience. These early raps incorporated the dozens, a product of African American culture. Kool Herc &

the Herculoids were the first Hip Hop group to gain recognition in New York citation needed, but the number of MC teams increased over time.

Often these were collaborations between former gangs, such as Afrikaa Bambaataa's Universal Zulu Nation - now an international organization. Melle Mel, a rapper with The Furious Five is often credited with being the first rap lyricist to call himself an "MC." During the early 1970s B-boying arose during block parties, as b-boys and b-girls got in front of the audience to dance in a distinctive and frenetic style. The style was documented for release to a world wide audience for the first time in documentaries and movies such as Style Wars, Wild Style, and Beat Street. The term "B-boy" was coined by DJ Kool Herc to describe the people who would wait for the break section of the song, getting in front of the audience to dance in a distinctive, frenetic style.

Although there were many early MCs that recorded solo projects of note, such as DJ Hollywood, Kurtis Blow and Spoonie Gee, the frequency of solo artists didn't increase until later with the rise of soloists with stage presence and drama, such as LL Cool J. Most early hip hop was dominated by groups where collaboration between the members was integral to the show. An example would be the early hip Hop group Funky Four Plus One, who performed in such a manner on Saturday Night Live in 1981. Hip Hop music was an outlet and a "voice" for the disenfranchised youth of low-economic areas as the culture reflected the social, economic and political realities of their lives.

INFLUENCE OF DISCO

Hip Hop music was influenced by disco and there was a backlash against it from its fans. According to Kurtis Blow, the early days of hip Hop were characterized by divisions between fans and detractors of disco music. Hip Hop had largely emerged as "a direct response to the watered down, Europeanised, disco music that permeated the airwaves", and the earliest hip hop was mainly based on hard funk loops. However, by 1979, disco instrumental loops/tracks had become the basis of much hip hop. The genre got the name, "disco rap". Ironically, Hip Hop was also a proponent in the eventual decline in disco's popularity.

DJ Pete Jones, Eddie Cheeba, DJ Hollywood, and

Love Bug Starski were disco-influenced hip hop DJs. Their styles differed from other hip hop musicians who focused on rapid-fire rhymes and more complex rhythmic schemes. Afrika Bambaataa, Paul Winley, Grandmaster Flash, and Bobby Robinson were all members of this latter group.

In Washington, D.C. go-go emerged as a reaction against disco and eventually incorporated characteristics of Hip Hop during the early 1980s. The genre of electronic music behaved similarly, eventually evolving into what is known as House Music in Chicago and Techno in New York. (Read my book: House Rules: Dance with Me on this subject.)

TRANSITION TO RECORDING

The first hip hop recording is widely regarded to be The Sugarhill Gang's "Rapper's Delight", from 1979. However, much controversy surrounds this allegation as some regard "King Tim III (Personality Jock)" by The Fatback Band, which was released a few weeks before "Rapper's Delight", as a rap record. There are various other claimants for the title of first hip Hop record.

By the early 1980s, all the major elements and techniques of the Hip Hop genre were in place. Though not yet mainstream, hip hop had permeated outside of New York City; it could be found in cities as diverse as Atlanta, Los Angeles, Washington, D.C., Baltimore, Dallas, Kansas City, San Antonio, Miami,

Seattle, St. Louis, New Orleans, Houston, and Toronto. Indeed, "Funk You Up" (1979), the first Hip Hop record released by a female group, and the second single released by Sugar Hill Records, was performed by The Sequence, a group from Columbia, South Carolina which featured Angie Stone.

Despite the genre's growing popularity, Philadelphia was, for many years, the only city whose contributions could be compared to New York City's. Hip hop music became popular in Philadelphia in the late 1970s. The first released record was titled "Rhythm Talk", by Jocko Henderson.

The New York Times had dubbed Philadelphia the "Graffiti Capital of the World" in 1971. Philadelphia native DJ Lady B recorded "To the Beat Y'All" in 1979, and became the first female solo hip hop artist to record music. Schoolly D, starting in 1984 and also from Philadelphia, began creating a style that would later be known as gangsta rap.

The 1980s marked the diversification of Hip Hop as the genre developed more complex styles. Early examples of the diversification process can be identified through such tracks as Grandmaster Flash's

"The Adventures of Grandmaster Flash on the Wheels of Steel" (1981), a single consisting entirely of sampled tracks as well as Afrika Bambaataa's "Planet Rock" (1982), which signified the fusion of hip Hop music with electro. In addition, Rammellzee & K-Rob's "Beat Bop" (1983) was a 'slow jam' which had a dub influence with its use of reverb and echo as texture and playful sound effects. The mid-1980s was marked by the influence of rock music, with the release of such albums as King of Rock and Licensed to Ill.

Heavy usage of the new generation of drum machines such as the Oberheim DMX and Roland 808 models was a characteristic of many 1980s songs. To this day, the 808-kickdrum is traditionally used by hip hop producers. Over time sampling technology became more advanced; however, earlier producers such as Marley Marl used drum machines to construct their beats from small excerpts of other beats in synchronisation, in his case, triggering 3 Korg sampling-delay units through a 808. Later, samplers such as the E-mu SP-1200 allowed not only more memory but more flexibility for creative production. This allowed the filtration and layering different hits, and with a possibility of re-sequencing them into a single piece.

With the emergence of a new generation of samplers such as the AKAI S900 in the late 1980s, producers did not require the aid of tape loops. Public Enemy's first album was created with the help of large tape loops. The process of looping break into a breakbeat now became more common with a sampler, now doing the job which so far had been done manually by the DJ. In 1989, DJ Mark James under the moniker "45 King", released "The 900 Number", a breakbeat track created by synchronizing samplers and vinyl.

The lyrical content of hip hop evolved as well. The early styles presented in the 1970s soon were replaced with metaphorical lyrics over more complex, multi-layered instrumentals. Artists such as Melle Mel, Rakim, Chuck D, and KRS-One revolutionized hip Hop by transforming it into a more mature art form. The influential single "The Message" (1982) by Grandmaster Flash and the Furious Five is widely considered to be the pioneering force for conscious rap.

During the early 1980s, electro music was fused with

elements of the hip hop movement, largely led by artists such as Cybotron, Hashim, Planet Patrol and Newcleus. The most notable proponent was Afrika Bambaataa who produced the single "Planet Rock".

Some rappers eventually became mainstream pop performers. Kurtis Blow's appearance in a Sprite commercial marked the first hip Hop musician to represent a major product. The 1981 song "Christmas Wrapping" by the new-wave band The Waitresses was one of the first pop songs to use some rapping in the delivery.

NATIONALIZATION & INTERNATIONALIZATION

Prior to the 1980s, rap music was largely confined within the context of the United States. However, during the 1980s, it began its spread and became a part of the music scene in dozens of countries. In the early part of the decade, B-boying became the first aspect of hip hop culture to reachGermany, Japan, Australia and South Africa, where the crew Black Noise established the practice before beginning to rap later in the decade. Musician and presenter Sidney became France's first black TV presenter with his show H.I.P. H.O.P. which screened on TF1 during 1984, a first for the genre worldwide. Radio Nova helped launch other French stars including Dee Nasty whose 1984 album Paname City Rappin' along with compilations Rapattitude 1 and 2 contributed to a general awareness of Hip Hop in France.

Hip Hop has always kept a very close relationship with the Latino community in New York. DJ Disco Wiz and the Rock Steady Crew were among early innovators from Puerto Rico. combining English and Spanish in the lyrics. The Mean Machine recorded their first song under the label "Disco Dreams" in 1981, while Kid Frost from Los Angeles began his career in 1982.

Cypress Hill was formed in 1988 in the suburb of South Gate outside Los Angeles when Senen Reyes (born in Havana) and his younger brother Ulpiano Sergio (Mellow Man Ace) moved from Cuba to South Gate with his family in 1971. They teamed up with DVX from Queens (New York), Lawrence Muggerud (DJ Muggs) and Louis Freese (B-Real), a Mexican/Cuban-American native of Los Angeles. After the departure of "Ace" to begin his solo career the group adopted the name of Cypress Hill named after a street running through a neighborhood nearby in South Los Angeles.

Hip hop in Japan is said to have begun when Hiroshi Fujiwara returned to Japan and started playing Hip-

Hop records in the early 1980s. The Japanese genre tends to be most directly influenced by America's old school, taking from the era's catchy beats, dance culture, while adding a carefree approach in incorporating it into their own. As a result, Hip Hop stands as one of the most commercially viable mainstream music genres in Japan, and the line between it and pop music is frequently blurred.

EARLY NEW SCHOOL

The new school of Hip Hop was the second wave of hip hop music, originating in 1983–84 with the early records of Run-D.M.C. and LL Cool J. As with the hip hop preceding it, the new school came predominately from New York City. The new school was initially characterized in form by drum machine-led minimalism, with influences from rock music. It was notable for taunts and boasts about rapping, and socio-political commentary, both delivered in an aggressive, self-assertive style. I

n image as in song, its artists projected a tough, cool, street b-boy attitude. These elements contrasted sharply with the funk and disco influenced outfits, novelty hits, live bands, synthesizers and party rhymes of artists prevalent prior to 1984, and rendered them old-school. New school artists made shorter songs that could more easily gain radio play, and more cohesive LPs than their old school counterparts.

By 1986, their releases began to establish the Hip Hop album as a fixture of the mainstream. Hip Hop music became commercially successful, as exemplified by the Beastie Boys' 1986 album, "Licensed to Ill," which was the first rap album to hit the Billboard charts.

THE GOLDEN AGE

Hip Hop's "golden age" (or "golden era") is a name given to a period in mainstream Hip Hop—usually cited as between the mid 1980s and the mid 1990s—said to be characterized by its diversity, quality, innovation and influence. There were strong themes ofAfrocentricity and political militancy, while the music was experimental and the sampling, eclectic. There was often a strong jazz influence. The artists most often associated with the phrase are Public Enemy, Boogie Down Productions, Eric B. & Rakim, De La Soul, A Tribe Called Quest, Gang Starr, Big Daddy Kane and the Jungle Brothers.

The golden age is noted for its innovation – a time "when it seemed that every new single reinvented the genre" according to Rolling Stone. Referring to "hip-hop in its golden age", Spin's editor-in-chief Sia Michel says, "there were so many important, groundbreaking albums coming out right about that time", and MTV's Sway Calloway adds: "The thing that made that era so great is that nothing was contrived. Everything was still being discovered and everything was still innovative and new". Writer William Jelani Cobb says "what made the era they inaugurated worthy of the term golden was the sheer number of stylistic innovations that came into existence... in these golden years, a critical mass of mic prodigies were literally creating themselves and their art form at the same time".

The specific time period that the golden age covers varies slightly from different sources. Some place it square in the 1980s and 1990s – Rolling Stone refers to "rap's '86-'99 golden age", and MSNBC states, "the "Golden Age" of Hip-Hop music: The '80s" and '90s".

GANGSTA RAP & WEST COAST

Gangsta rap is a subgenre of Hip-Hop that reflects the violent stories and lifestyles of inner-city youths. Gangsta is a non-rhotic pronunciation of the word "gangster." The genre was pioneered in the mid 1980s by rappers such as Schooly D and Ice T, and was popularized in the later part of the 1980s by groups like N.W.A. Ice-T released "6 in the Mornin'", which is often regarded as the first gangsta rap song, in 1986. After the national attention that Ice-T and N.W.A created in the late 1980s and early 1990s, gangsta rap became the most commercially lucrative subgenre of hip hop.

N.W.A is the group most frequently associated with

pioneering gangsta rap. Their lyrics were more violent, openly confrontational, and shocking than those of established rap acts, featuring incessant profanity and, controversially, use of the word "nigger". These lyrics were placed over rough, rock guitar-driven beats, contributing to the music's hard-edged feel. The first blockbuster gangsta rap album was N.W.A's Straight Outta Compton, released in 1988. Straight Outta Compton would establish West Coast hip hop as a vital genre, and establish Los Angeles as a legitimate rival to hip hop's long-time capital, New York City. Straight Outta Compton sparked the first major controversy regarding hip hop lyrics when their song "Fuck Tha Police" earned a letter from FBI Assistant Director, Milt Ahlerich, strongly expressing law enforcement's resentment of the song. Due to the influence of Ice T and N.W.A, gangsta rap is often credited as being an originally West Coast phenomenon, despite the contributions of East Coast acts like Boogie Down Productions in shaping the genre.

The subject of gangsta rap has caused a great deal of controversy over the years. Criticism has come from both left and right-wing commentators, politicians and religious leaders. Gangsta rappers often find themselves defending their actions by saying that they are describing the reality of inner-city life, and that they are only adopting a character, like an actor playing a role, thus behaving in ways that they may not necessarily endorse.

WORLD HIP HOP

In Haiti, Hip-Hop was developed in the early 1980s, and is mostly accredited to Master Dji and his songs "Vakans" and "Politik Pam". What later became known as "Rap Kreyòl" grew in popularity in the late 1990s with King Posse and Original Rap Stuff. Due to cheaper recording technology and flows of equipment to Haiti, more Rap Kreyòl groups are recording songs, even after the January 12th earthquake.

In the Dominican Republic, a recording by Santi Y Sus Duendes and Lisa M became the first single of merenrap, a fusion of Hip Hop and merengue.

New York City experienced a heavy Jamaican hip-hop influence during the 1990s. This influence was brought on by cultural shifts particularly because of the heightened immigration of Jamaicans to New York City and the American-born Jamaican youth who were coming of age during the 1990s. Rap artists such as De La Soul and Black Star have produced albums influenced by Jamaican roots.

In Europe, Africa, and Asia, Hip-Hop began to move from the underground to mainstream audiences and was the domain of both ethnic nationals and immigrants. British hip hop, for example, became a genre of its own and spawned many artists such as Wiley, Dizzee Rascal, The Streets and many more.

Germany produced the well-known "Die Fantastischen Vier" as well as several Turkish performers like the controversial Cartel, Kool Savaş, and Azad. Similarly,

France has produced a number of native-born stars, MC Solaar, Rohff, Rim'K or Booba. In the Netherlands, important nineties rappers include The Osdorp Posse, a crew from Amsterdam, Extince, from Oosterhout, and Postmen.

Italy found its own rappers, including Jovanotti and Articolo, grow nationally renowned, while the

Polish scene began in earnest early in the decade with the rise of PM Cool Lee.

In Romania, B.U.G. Mafia came out of Bucharest's Pantelimon neighborhood, and their brand of gangsta rap underlines the parallels between life in Romania's Communist-era apartment blocks and in the housing projects of America's ghettos.

Israel and Palestinian Hip Hop grew greatly in popularity at the end of the decade, with several stars including Palestinian rapper (Tamer Nafer) and Israeli (Subliminal) hitting the scenes.

In Asia, mainstream stars rose to prominence in the Philippines, led by Francis Magalona, Rap Asia, MC Lara and Lady Diane. In Japan, where underground rappers had previously found a limited audience, and popular teen idols brought a style called J-rap to the top of the charts in the middle of the 1990s.

Latinos had played an integral role in the early development of hip hop, and the style had spread to parts of Latin America, such as Cuba, early in its history. In Mexico, popular hip hop began with the success of Calo [disambiguation needed] in the early 1990s. Later in the decade, with Hispanic rap groups like Cypress Hill gained fame on the American music charts while Mexican rap rock groups, such as Control Machete, rose to prominence in their country. An annual Cuban Hip Hop concert held at Alamar in Havana helped popularize Cuban hip hop, beginning in 1995. Hip Hop grew steadily more popular in Cuba, mainly because of official governmental support for all musicians.

The Brazilian hip hop scene is considered to be the second biggest in the world, just behind American hip Hop. It is heavily associated with racial and economic inequalities in the country, where a lot of blacks live in poverish situations in the violent slums, known in Brazil as favelas. São Paulo is where hip hop began in the country, but it soon spread all over Brazil, and today, almost every big Brazilian city, such as Rio de Janeiro, Salvador, Curitiba, Porto Alegre, Belo Horizonte, Recife and Brasilia, has a hip hop scene.

Racionais MC's, MV Bill, Marcelo D2, Rappin Hood, Jay Nano, Thaíde and Dj Hum, Bonde do Tigrão, Bonde do Rolê, GOG, RZO are considered the most powerful names in Brazilian hip hop music industry.

GLIMPSES OF WEST COAST HIP HOP

After N.W.A broke up, Dr. Dre released The Chronic in 1992, which peaked at #1 on the R&B/hip hop chart, on the pop chart and spawned a pop single with "Nuthin' but a "G" Thang." The Chronic took West Coast rap in a new direction, influenced strongly by P funk artists, melding sleazy funk beats with slowly drawled lyrics. This came to be known as G-funk and dominated mainstream hip Hop for several years through a roster of artists on Death Row Records, including Tupac Shakur, whose single "To Live & Die in LA" was a big hit, andSnoop Dogg, whose Doggystyle included the songs "What's My Name" and "Gin and Juice," both top ten hits.

Detached from this scene, were other artists such as

Freestyle Fellowship, The Pharcyde as well as more underground artists such as the Solesides collective (DJ Shadow and Blackalicious amongst others) Jurassic, Ugly Duckling (hip hop group), People Under the Stairs, The Alkaholiks, and earlier,Souls of Mischief represented a return to the roots of sampling and well-planned rhyme schemes. Also, the west coast has *avant-garde* Hip Hop label known as the Anticon, where artist such as Dose One, Sole (artist), and many others make experimental Hip Hop that goes beyond the status quo.

GLIMPSES OF EAST COAST HIP HOP

- In the early 1990s, East Coast hip hop was dominated by the Native Tongues posse which was loosely composed of De La Soul with producer Prince Paul, A Tribe Called Quest, The Jungle Brothers, as well as their loose affiliates - 3rd Bass, Main Source, and the less successful Black Sheep & KMD. Although originally a *"daisy age"* conception stressing the positive aspects of life, darker material (such as De La Soul's thought-provoking "Millie Pulled a Pistol on Santa") soon crept in.

- Artists such as Masta Ace (particularly for SlaughtaHouse) & Brand Nubian, Public Enemy, Organized Konfusion had a more overtly militant pose, both in sound and manner. Biz Markie, the "clown prince of hip hop", was causing himself and all other hip-hop producers a problem with his appropriation of the Gilbert O'Sullivan song "Alone again, naturally".

- In the mid-1990s, artists such as the Wu-Tang Clan, Nas and The Notorious B.I.G. increased New York's visibility at a time when hip hop was mostly dominated by West Coast artists. The mid to late 1990s saw a generation of rappers such as the members of D.I.T.C. such as the late Big L and Big Pun.

- The productions of RZA, particularly for Wu-Tang Clan, became influential with artists such as Mobb Deep due to the combination of somewhat detached instrumental loops, highly compressed and processed drums and gangsta lyrical content. Wu-Tang affiliate albums such as Raekwon the Chef's Only Built 4 Cuban Linx and GZA's Liquid Swords are now viewed as classics along with Wu-Tang "core" material.

- Producers such as DJ Premier (primarily for Gangstarr but also for other affiliated artists such as

Jeru the Damaja), Pete Rock (With CL Smooth and supplying beats for many others), Buckwild, Large Professor, Diamond D and The 45 King supplying beats for numerous MCs regardless of location.

- Albums such as Nas's Illmatic, Jay-Z's Reasonable Doubt and O.C.'s Word...Life are made up of beats from this pool of producers.

- Later in the decade, the business acumen of the Bad Boy Records tested itself against Jay-Z and his Roc-A-Fella Records and, on the West Coast, Death Row Records.

- The rivalry between the East Coast and the West Coast rappers eventually turned personal, aided in part by the music media.

- Although the "big business" end of the market dominated matters commercially the late 1990s to early 2000s saw a number of relatively successful East Coast indie labels such as Rawkus Records (with whom Mos Def gained great success) and later Def Jux; the history of the two labels is intertwined, the latter having been started by EL-P of Company Flow in reaction to the former, and offered an outlet for more underground artists such as Mike Ladd, Aesop Rock, Mr Lif, RJD2, Cage and Cannibal Ox. Other acts such as the Hispanic Arsonists and slam poet turned MC Saul Williams met with differing degrees of success.

DIVERSIFICATION OF STYLES

In the late 1990s, the styles of Hip Hop diversified. Southern rap became popular in the early 1990s, with the releases of Arrested Development's "3 Years, 5 Months & 2 Days in the Life Of... " in 1992, Goodie Mob's "Soul Food", in 1995 and OutKast's "ATLiens" in 1996. All three groups were from Atlanta, Georgia. Later, Master P (Ghetto D) built up a roster of artists (the No Limit posse) based out of New Orleans, Master P Incorporated. Rap groups with G-Funk and Miami bass along with other distinctive sounds from St. Louis, Chicago, Washington D.C., Detroit and other big cities gained popularity.

In the 1990s, elements of hip hop continued to be assimilated into other genres of popular music. Neo

Soul, for example, combined hip hop and soul music.

In the 1980s and 1990s, rapcore, rap rock and rap metal, fusions of hip hop and hardcore punk, rock and heavy metal became popular genres of rap music among mainstream audiences. Rage Against the Machine and Limp Bizkit were among the most well-known bands who played across these genres.

Digable Planets' 1993 release Reachin' (A New Refutation of Time and Space) was an influential jazz rap record sampling the likes of Don Cherry, Sonny Rollins, Art Blakey, Herbie Mann, Herbie Hancock, Grant Green, and Rahsaan Roland Kirk. It spawned the hit single "Rebirth of Slick (Cool Like Dat)" which reached 16 on the Billboard Hot 100.

White rappers like the Beastie Boys, House of Pain and 3rd Bass had had some popular success or critical acceptance from the Hip-Hop colored community, but Eminem's success, in 1999 with the platinum "The Slim Shady LP," surprised many in the ghettos.

The popularity of hip hop music continued through the 2000s. In the year 2000, "The Marshall Mathers

LP" by Eminem sold over ten million copies in the United States and was the fastest-selling hip hop album of all time while Nelly's debut LP, "Country Grammar," sold over nine million. In the 2000s, crunk music, a derivative of Southern hip hop, gained considerable popularity via the likes of Lil Jon and the Ying Yang Twins.

Hip hop influences also found their way increasingly into mainstream pop during this period mainly the mid 2000s. In the East Coast, pop acts with hip-hop ventures grew tremendously.

The United States also saw the success of alternative hip hop from groups like The Roots, Dilated Peoples, Gnarls Barkley and Mos Def, who achieved significant recognition. Gnarls Barkley's album, "St. Elsewhere," which contained a fusion of funk, neo soul and hip hop, had debuted at number #20 on the Billboard 200 Chart.

ACROSS THE WORLD

The continuation of hip hop can also be seen in different national contexts. In Tanzania, maintained popular acts of their own in the early 2000s, infusing local styles of Afrobeat and arabesque melodies, dancehall and hip-hop beats, and Swahili lyrics. Scandinavian, especially Danish and Swedish, performers became well known outside of their country, while Hip Hop continued its spread into new regions, including Russia, Japan, Philippines, Canada, China, Korea, India and especially Vietnam. Of particular importance is the influence on East Asian nations, where hip hop music has become fused with local popular music to form different styles such as K-pop, C-pop and J-pop.

In the Netherlands, MC Brainpower went from being an underground battle rapper to mainstream recognition in the Benelux, thus influencing numerous rap artists in the region. In Israel, rapper Subliminal reaches out to Israeli youth with political and religious-themed lyrics, usually with a Zionist message.One of the countries outside the US where Hip-Hop is most popular is the United Kingdom. In the 2000s a derivative genre from Hip-Hop (as well as UK Garage and Drum and Bass) known as Grime became popular with artists such as Dizzee Rascal becoming successful. Although it is immensely popular, many British politicians criticize the music for what they see as promoting theft and murder, similar to gangsta rap in America. These criticisms have been deemed racist by the mostly Black British grime industry. Despite its controversial nature, grime has had a major affect on British fashion and pop music, with many young working class youth emulating the clothing worn by grime stars like Dizzee Rascal and Wiley. There are many subgenres of grime, including Rhythm and Grime, a mix of R&B and grime, and grindie, a mix of indie rock and grime popularized by indie rock band Hadouken.

Rap has globalized into many cultures worldwide, as

evident through the emergence of numerous regional scenes. It has emerged globally as a movement based upon the main tennets of hip hop culture. The music and the art continue to embrace, even celebrate, its transnational dimensions while staying true to the local cultures to which it is rooted. Hip-hop's inspiration differs depending on each culture. Still, the one thing virtually all Hip Hop artists worldwide have in common is that they acknowledge their debt to those African American people in New York who launched the global movement. While hip-hop is sometimes taken for granted by Americans, it is not so elsewhere, especially in the developing world, where it has come to represent the empowerment of the disenfranchised and a slice of the American dream. American Hip-Hop music has reached the cultural corridors of the globe and has been absorbed and reinvented around the world.

GLITCH HOP AND WONKY MUSIC

Glitch Hop and Wonky music evolved following the rise of Trip Hop, dubstep and IDM. Both styles of music frequently reflect the experimental nature of IDM and the heavy bass featured in dubstep songs. While trip hop was described as being a distinct British upper-middle class take on Hip-Hop, glitch-hop and wonky music have featured much more stylistic diversity. Both genres are melting pots of influence, echoes of 1980s pop music, Indian ragas, eclectic jazz and West Coast rap can be heard in glitch Hop productions. Los Angeles, London, Glasgow and a number of other cities have become hot spots for these scenes, and underground scenes have developed across the world in smaller communities. Both genres often pay homage to more well older and more well established electronic music artists such as Radiohead, Aphex Twin and Boards of Canada as well as independent hip hop producers like J Dilla and Madlib.

Glitch Hop is a fusion genre of hip hop and glitch music that originated in the early to mid 2000s in the United States and Europe. Musically, it is based on irregular, chaotic breakbeats, glitchy basslines and other typical sound effects used in glitch music, like skips. Glitch Hop artists include Prefuse Dabrye and Flying Lotus.

CRUNK AND SNAP MUSIC

Crunk originated from southern hip hop in the late 1990s. The style was pioneered and commercialized by artists from Memphis, Tennessee and Atlanta, Georgia.

Looped, stripped-down drum machine rhythms are usually used. The Roland TR-808 and 909 are among the most popular. The drum machines are usually accompanied by simple, repeated synthesizer melodies and heavy bass stabs. The tempo of the music is somewhat slower than hip-hop, around the speed of reggaeton.

The focal point of crunk is more often the beats and music than the lyrics therein. Crunk rappers, however, often shout and scream their lyrics, creating an aggressive, almost heavy, style of hip-hop. While other subgenres of hip-hop address sociopolitical or personal concerns, crunk is almost exclusively party music, favoring call and response hip-hop slogans in lieu of more substantive approaches.

ABOUT THE AUTHOR

Eric Reese was born and raised in Philadelphia, Pennsylvania, USA. Raised in the era of the start of Hip Hop, he's one of the genre's biggest fans.

Don't forget to grab Volume 2 & 3

Join my email list, media inquiries or drop a testimonial

email: feekness@gmail.com
website: http://eric-reese.com

Printed in the USA
CPSIA information can be obtained
at www.ICGtesting.com
LVHW011637210823
755861LV00004B/20